"The more man|woman meditates on good thoughts, the better will be his|her world and the world at large."
-Confucius

Onward I go
Journey into the soul
Good Thoughts I must hear
Good Thoughts I must know
Good Thoughts I must share
For the world
To know

Love to write, pen in hand, scribbling ink onto page, motions transcribe thoughts into physical form. Writing is a connection, a bridge to the divine infinite intelligence openly available to us all. This written journey will be a collection of attempts to hack into the source of knowledge, the higher mind, the collective consciousness, and ask it this question?

What good thoughts do you have for the world today?

We shall then bring back its messages
::::::::::::::::::::::::::::::

Good Thoughts

Life is limitless. Always an infinite number of parallel realities one decision away. Jump I say, all you who dare, into a new vision, a new decision, for your life.

When making the choice, choose the third way. First only you will see one & two extremes. Then lying in between, thee shall see, a middle way, a middle path, that balances both extremes.

"The middle path is the way to wisdom." -Rumi

Life is meaningless. Find freedom in that.
Freedom to choose...knock...knock...what matters
in your life. Freedom to seek, find, and give
meaning to that which moves you.

Quantum physics says we are co-creators of our
world. With what exactly we do not know,
consciousness may be the connection.

Look at the world around you,
that which you helped co-create.

What do you see...
Notice life is moving...
Where do you wish it to go?

Find and give meaning to that.
Imprint your energy on the world.
Live meaningful.

"Life has no meaning. Each of us has meaning and
we bring it to life. It is a waste to be asking the
question, when you are the answer. "
-Joseph Campbell

Welcome to the uncertain present and future. Limitations lie in perception. Invite the uncertain future with good intentions. A warm greeting the mirror shall always return. Allow the present, the feelings, sensations, emotions.

Know in all times
This Too Shall Pass
Nothing has come to stay and that is ok.
We are the ever present
And the ever changing.

"Faith is a place of mystery, where we find the courage to believe in what we cannot see and the strength to let go of our fear of uncertainty."
–Brene Brown

Be still...
Tap into the flow of life energy
Breathe...
Inhale prana energy
Look into nature

See the ease in which it lives, provides, and is provided for. Does the universe not take care of you in this way?

If you are living...
Are the resources for life not within you?
You are the song and the dance.
You are the wave and the ocean.
Life lives within you, within the Earth, the Cosmos, the Universe.

Tune into the connection.

"The cosmos is within us, we're made of star stuff. We are a way for the cosmos to know itself." -Carl Sagan

Good Thoughts

5

ANYTHING IS POSSIBLE

Every thought passing through your brain...
work with them...attention...
Energy goes where attention flows.
What do you believe is possible?
What do you see that is not yet manifest?
What life do you Invision yourself living?
Is there a process to get there?
Yes? Go!
No? Go!

No matter where you go or what you seek,
what you will always find,
is what you believe is possible for you.

"Whatever you hold in your mind will tend to occur
in your life. If you continue to believe as you have
always believed, you will continue to act as you
have always acted. If you continue to act as you
have always acted, you will continue to get what
you have always gotten. If you want different
results in your life or your work, all you have to do
is change your mind."

Allow
Allow life to happen
Surrender
Strong word
Powerful
Change is inevitable, it is constant.
Control what you can control,
surrender the unknown.
You are a participant in the game of
known & unknown.
Find your balance...a way of living that works
for you. Apply energy to good
thoughts & actions.
Create productive habits.
Life is a day by day quest.
Set sail for a beautiful future.
A charted course.
No stone destination.

"No valid plans for the future can be made by
those who have no capacity for living now."
-Alan Watts

Good Thoughts

It is like waking up on a cold morning. The energy and determination needed to pull the covers off, face the environment, and boldy plant your feet on the ground...
That burst of will power can change your life

Use it to harness good opportunity at a moments notice. Use it to apply daily the energy necessary to follow through on productive habits. Use it to stop bad habits in their tracks and never return. Use it for the ability to walk away from bad vibes.

Utilize your power
Inhance your life
Level Up

"Everything changes when you start to emit your own frequency rather than absorbing the frequencies around you. When you start imprinting your intent on the universe rather than receiving an imprint from existence."
-Barbara Marciniak

Good Thoughts

Imagine
Miracles
Imagine
How beautiful life can be
practice practice practice
In the mind first you see
Internally you find desires
External you wish them to be
Manifest a vision
Paint with the mind's eye
Ground the emotions
Feelings of future living
Into the present time.

"If you believe the doubts in your mind, you won't achieve the dreams in your heart." –Terri Savelle Foy

Listen
Watch your words
Hear them
Do you like what they are saying?
Do they speak life or death?
Create or destroy?

There is power in the tongue
Manifestation in the echos
What words are you vibrating out into
the world...

Speak love, peace, joy, calm,
understanding into the world. Let your
words be words of healing and
positivity.

"Let your speech always be with grace."
-Colossians 4:6

Love
Unconditional love
It's a way of being
It's a state of being
Bypassing all preconceived differences
and living without judgment.
Be present and grateful in the presence
of all life. Look deeply into another
humans eyes, or any animal you
interact with, connect with the life
essence, the light inside. Stare into
nature, the connected web of life. At the
subatomic level all life is made up of the
same stuff. You are a part of the whole.

"If you see yourself in others, then
whom can you harm." –Buddha

Time is precious.
Spend it wisely.
Give it to people you care about, people you love. No matter how bright or dull a moment, if it is with those people whom you cherish, the time was spent correctly. You must not waste the valuable time in bad environments, around negative people. Be strong when you need to leave, to say no, to walk away. You choose where to spend your energy, don't let it be drained away.

"Walk away from anything that gives you bad vibes. There is no need to make sense of it. It is your life. Do what makes you happy."

1 2

Mind
Body
Connection
You experience life through so many senses.
Exercise all of them.
Meditate
Work out and stress relief for the brain
muscle. Exercise the body, challenge yourself
physically. Open the energy. Connect with
the Earth.
Grounded.
Mentally and Physically rooted.
Healing is released from within.
The power that made the body,
heals the body.

"No man|woman has the right to be an
amateur in the matter of physical training. It
is a shame for a man|woman to grow old
without seeing the beauty and strength of
which his|her body is capable." –Socrates

Good Thoughts

1 3

Take time for children
If they seek your attention
Slow down
Be grateful
Give fully your attention
Enjoy the warp of timelessness
In those moments
The universe is calm
Learn from each other
Kids are the future
Always will be

They can show you a new way of seeing the world, a new perspective.
You can share a wealth of information and experience, the knowledge you've gathered further down life's path. Exchange.

"I believe that children are our future. Teach them well and let them lead the way. Show them all the beauty they possess inside."
–Whitney Houston

Good Thoughts

Get comfortable with yourself.
Feel good inside your own skin.
Find love in solitude.
Treat yourself with the highest standards.
You can't fool you, only pretend to.
Ask yourself questions.
Hear the silence.
Then hear the answers.
You can trust you.
You know what to do.
If necessary what needs to be done.
Go in the direction you guide yourself.

"You can seek the advice of others, surround yourself with trusted advisors. But in the end, the decision is always yours and yours alone. And when it is time to act and you're all alone with your back against the wall. The only voice that matters is the one in your head. The one telling you what you already knew. The one that's almost always right."
-Meredith Grey

Good Thoughts

Notice your weaknesses
Feel weak...it's ok...it's alright
Soon after you will know real strength
Conquer yourself
Make personal improvements
Growth is a daily commitment
Change happens
Use it to your advantage
Don't hang your head on days of dread
When you feel you could have done more,
not wasted your time...
lived better.
These days are important too.
Life is a puzzle of many days.
Notice your holes,
the pieces return back to you.

"You cannot let go of anything if you cannot
notice that you are holding it. Admit your
weaknesses and watch them morph into
your greatest strengths."
–Neale Donald Walsch

1 6

You possess many gifts, passions,
purposes. You will walk many paths.
One step at a time.
What work? What idea? What gift?
Do you have that can better the world.
Dream big. Work small.

Life is a gift you have been given. Also a
gift you'll leave generations to follow.
All humans & life inherit the Earth.
Leave it better than you found it.

"Life is a gift, never take that for
granted."

Deal with it, you don't know where you're going.
What will happen next?
Who will you meet?
What events will shape your life?
That's all good.
Move in the direction of your desires.
Follow the path.
Trust in its next step.
Up around the bend
Treasures are found
You might have missed
If you stayed in the crown
Your head...the mind

Don't be caged by expectations of futures still to come, you never know what it's going to be, so don't worry so much, you see?!

False. Evidence. Appearing. Real.

"Courage is resistance to fear, mastery of fear, not absence of fear." –Mark Twain

"What you are afraid to do is a clear indication of the next thing you need to do." –Ralph Waldo Emerson

1 8

Welcome to the heart field
It's all around you
Surrounds you
Extends outward
Radiates out from your heart
Your heart is powerful
Intelligent
Send out good, positive, conscious, heartfelt vibes
to the universe. Your heartfield directly impacts the
world around you and ripples off into infinity.

Give loving emotions,
to the world from where you sit.
Don't underestimate its effect.

"When we form heart-centered beliefs within our
bodies, in the language of physics we're creating
the electrical and magnetic expression of them as
waves of energy, which aren't confined to our
hearts or limited by the physical barrier of our skin
and bones. So clearly we're speaking to the world
around us in each moment of every day through a
language that has no words: the belief waves of our
hearts." -Gregg Braden

When you gather together
When you look up into the sky
When you feel apart of something
Bigger than yourself
Waves of harmony
Spread around the Earth
Humans have limitless potential
When they work together
When they co-exist
The stars can be explored
The planet healed
Primitive issues food water shelter
Never a problem...provided....
New standards of living
Mental capacities freed
New level living
The animal inside
Feels no worry no fear
Mind above
Fight or flight

"I can do things you cannot, you can do things I can
not, together we can do great things."
-Mother Teresa

When life feels
Slow
Tiring
Repetitive
Seek new
New sights
Opportunities
People
Experiences
Embrace new opportunities
You have now outgrown an old version of you. That
old energy, old habits, old program, is outdated.
New energy is needed to sustain your new level.
Jump into new heart opening, heart pumping
moments. You now require more energy, more life.
So when life feels slow
When you feel small
Know your transcendence
Find the new you

"When she transformed into a butterfly, the
caterpillars spoke not of her beauty, but of her
weirdness. They wanted her to change back into
what she had always been...
But she had wings." -Dean Jackson

Good Thoughts

Every day begins anew
A fresh start
A clean slate
What a thought, to change your name?
Your name was given to you not chosen.
What new identity would you create
with a new name?
Just know that this ability to change everything,
to move in a new direction,
is available in every moment.
Also know your identity and your true self is
deeper even than the beliefs and feelings
associated with the sound of your name...

In every moment
Till your moment
of death
You have the ability to
Live love learn grow experience
And become more of yourself

"Identity is never static.
Always in the making and never made."

Good Thoughts

2 2

It may not happen right away
It is ok to catch yourself
Question yourself
Your words
Work till the point where every word spoken from
your mouth was chosen...conscious...
We re act
Respond
Say words we can't take back PAUSE
Before responding...pre meditate
Work till every word spoken is your honest truth
Listen to your own lies...learn from them
Find your truth
Your honesty
Speak it Act it Live it
Alignment

"Happiness is when what you think, what you say,
and what you do, are in harmony."
-Mahatma Gandhi

"Words reveal your beliefs and intentions. Action
reveals your character. When they are in alignment,
they reveal your greatest life."

2 3

Subconscious Programs
They run a part of your life
Become awake to your sleeping self
Beliefs thoughts limits fears habits words
They may not be yours
The mind is in a hypnotic receptive state
In developmental early years
You absorb everything you see, hear, and learn
Who taught you how to live?
Reobserve the way of life of those you observed as a child.
What of yourself can you find in them...
See the positive and negative attributes
Through non judgemental eyes
Your parents, guardians, teachers
Were brought up by others with
Old programs
No blame to be cast
Ways of living become outdated
New generations come with new software
New Knowledge
New ways of life
View the old programs
Still on display in your life
Don't carry any old baggage you do not want to.

"Everytime you are tempted to react in the same old way.
Ask if you want to be a prisoner of the past or a pioneer of
the future." -Deepak Chopra

Will Power
Your personal hammer and chisel
A gift since birth
Use it
Create a masterpiece of a life
Clank
Clank
Clank
Clank...
One swing at a time
Yes
It is that simple
Dream Big
Work small
Persist
Apply
Will

"You don't set out to build a wall. You don't say I'm going to build the biggest, baddest, greatest wall that's ever been built. You don't start there. You say. I'm going to lay this brick as perfectly as a brick can be laid. You do that every single day. And soon you have a wall."
-Will Smith

Good Thoughts

25

Your mind will wander
Gently reel it back
Focus is a muscle
It will get stronger
As you train it
Apply focus to your choice of work
In healthy habits & hobbies
Apply focus in your relationships
And your communication with other people
A present focused listener
Will easily make friends
So focus
On your life
Your family
Your passions
Yourself

Other times
Don't be afraid to let go of the reel
Let the mind think
You are strong enough to pull it back in

"You can't depend on your eyes,
When your imagination is out of focus."
-Mark Twain

2 6

You are free to be
Anything
Anyone
Don't be tentative to reinvent
If you feel pulled toward a new path
Walk there
Questioning the uncertainty
Thinking of answers for what others might say
Only slows you down from finding out for yourself
Engage in the new experience
Then decide
Then figure out if it is the right path
No matter what
You yourself have to be on it for the realization and
understanding to follow
So go where you wish
Do as you please
Be as you are
You will know what is right for you

"Trust yourself. Create the kind of self that you will
be happy to live with all your life. Make the most of
yourself by fanning the tiny, inner sparks of
possibility into flames of achievement."
-Golda Meir

Good Thoughts

27

Create mantras for yourself
Powerful words and phrases
Repeated internally or aloud
To help alter your vibration
From the inside out
When negative thoughts swirl
Around in your head
Use a mantra to dissolve the thought pattern
When you feel grateful
Use a mantra as a message of thanks
When meditating
Use a mantra to focus your thinking
When your body feels out of sorts
Use a mantra to re-align
Anytime
Use a mantra to send love
& light out to the universal field

"A mantra is nothing more than a collection of
words strung together to create a positive effect."
-Robin S Sharma

"So that's the power of mantra, because mantra
moves the elements - all five elements, plus
Heavens, plus Earth." -Yogi Bhajan

Take care of where you live
Keep clean your environment
The world is always a mirror
Look at yourself
When looking at your home
Are you neat and tidy
Or dusty and dirty
Is there clutter in your space?
Is there clutter in your mind?
Sometimes cleaning, letting go, getting rid of...
Takes the trash out of your life.
Make room for new
By clearing the old
Though sometimes
You must let go to let go
Not let go to get
See yourself
See the space you occupy
What in your world
Needs cleaning?

"The most important thing to understand is that
feng shui is really about the energy that's
surrounding you in your personal space."
-Lillian Too

Good Thoughts

2 9

What will you do?
When weighing your options...
Which will you choose?
How will you know it's the right choice?
Will you ever know...
Hard to say
So what can you do
Feel it out
What do the feelings in your body tell you?
If you care to share
Consult those closest to you
Life will lead you to many crossroads
Give yourself due time to analyze the options
Then move
Then decide
Knowing there are no wrong choices
You can re-evaluate when need be
Ultimately
There's only one way to find out
Hindsight

"Decisions are the hardest thing to make, especially
when it is a choice between where you should be
and where you want to be."

3 0

You have to love you
Truly
Internally
If there is no love
Inside of you
For you
There is no love to give
Nurture the relationship
Help it grow
Spend time with you
And you alone
When you can smile
When you can laugh
You created a path
Bridged the gap
Now there's space
For love to grow
Deep from within
Rooted to the soul

"Self respect, self worth and self love, all start with self.
Stop looking outside of yourself for your value."
- Rob Liano

"You are enough.
You have nothing to prove to anyone."
–Maya Angelou

Good Thoughts

Don't stress
It's not worth it
Wasted energy
Think & ponder on life's dilemmas
Give energy where it is needed
Stress & worry accomplish nothing but dis ease
Mental dis ease leads to physical dis ease
Stress & worry stem from a future not yet lived
Fear & worry about what might be
Come back to the present
Allow the day dream to become the nightmare
Say even if the worst possible outcome shall
happen
THIS TOO SHALL PASS

"Take a deep breath. Get present in the moment
and ask yourself what is important this very
second." -Greg Mckeown

"Your calm mind is the ultimate weapon against
your challenges. So relax" -Bryant Mcgill

You can keep your secrets if you want to
Carry them all the way to the grave
If you can handle the weight
Otherwise
Let it go
Set yourself free
Say what you need to say
Tell who you must tell
Or confide with who you can trust
Truly
If you can't handle it
Let it out
That will help everyone involved
If you think it will hurt others
Carry it
You're strong
We all die with secrets
Just don't overload yourself

"How long will this go on?"
Asked my diary.
"What will go on?"
"For how long will I have to bear the weight of your
secrets, your internal verses and inner turbulence?"
"Until there's none left inside me."
–The Drifter

Thank You
A powerful prayer
A blessing
A mantra in itself
A gift of serenity to the universe
Give vocal thanks as often as possible
And continuously in your mind
Vibrate thanks
Operate from a thankful state of being

"A hundred times a day I remind myself that my inner and outer life depend on the labors of other men, living and dead, and that I must exert myself in order to give in the measure as I have received and am still receiving." -Albert Einstein

"Gratitude can transform common days into thanksgiving, turn routine jobs into joy, and change ordinary opportunities into blessings." -William A Ward

You're not that hungry
You're not starving
Even if you say so
You know what I mean?
Eat consciously
Thoughtful
Plan your meal
Create your dish
Make it yourself
Know what's in there
No need to blindly consume
Food is energy
Food can heal & sustain health
Eat for nutrients
Pass above the primitive mindset
Food is not scarce
The necessary agriculture can be moved indoors
and provide the world with a whole foods plant based diet.
Hunger Eradicated
A time will come when the world will see
Animal death is no longer required for
Human Survival

"The time will come when man such as I will look upon the murder of animals as they now look upon the murder of men." -Leonardo Da Vinci

"I am not so important that another living being should have to die for me."

35

Entheogens
Plant medicines
Will play a major role
In the advancement of
Human consciousness...
They already have

"I believe that used responsibly and in a mature way, the entheogens mediate access to the numinous dimensions of existence, have a great healing and transformative potential, and represent a tool for spiritual development."
-Stanislav Grof

"Ayahuasca is not a drug in the western sense, something you take to get rid of something. Properly used, it opens up parts of yourself that you usually have no access to. The parts of the brain that hold emotional memories come together with those parts that modulate insight and awareness, so you see past experiences in a new way."
-Dr Gabor Mate

"Plant spirit medicine is the Shaman's way with plants. It recognizes that plants have spirit and that spirit is the strongest medicine. Spirit can heal the deepest reaches of the heart & soul."
-Eliot Cowan

Good Thoughts

3 6

Don't neglect the inner child
The innocent you
Think back on what you enjoyed
In your younger years
What were your strengths?
What were you good at?
Indulge in these things
Act in ways that remind you of the joys
In a time that once was real
You are an older & wiser
Human being now
With more potential than a child
More well equipped to handle the world
Inside of you though is a place
A place where you see with no judgment
And absorb the newness
Of the world around you
There's a child inside
That still wishes to play
So play

"We have to listen to the child we once were, the child who still exists inside us. That child understands magic moments. We can stifle its cries, but we cannot silence its voice. The child we once were is still there." -Paulo Coelho

Exercise your mind
Read
Learn
Use your muscle
Watch it grow
Reshape the neuroplasticity
Light up the neurotransmitters
Rewrite the subconscious program
Upgrade the conscious hardware
Challenge the mind to keep
Reading & Thinking
Pondering Life
Stay with the world
It is your job
Keep up with the times
Keep your mind up to speed

"If you exercise your mind you're not going to get sick." -Rob Walton

Nobody is perfect
No thing is perfect
No moment
No outcome
Leave room for imperfection
Leave room for growth
What happens outside your
Expectations
Might be
What is meant
To Be

"Trade your expectations for
appreciation and your whole world
changes in an instant."
-Tony Robbins

Transcend your surroundings
Transcend your environment
"In the world, but not of it."
Attune the internal state of being
To your choosing
Then approach the world
Grounded
Unwavering
Unshakeable
Flexible
Rooted in vibration
If you approached the world, life, people
with compassion.
How different would your life be?
What should you change?

"Love is a state of being. Your love is not
outside; it is deep within you. You can never
lose it, and it cannot leave you."
-Eckhart Tolle

Life energy cultivation is a lifelong commitment. Your diet and consumption should prep you with good energy. You may experience being drained and tired. Something lead you there. Aid the movement of energy throughout the body with physical exercise and actions. Energy is within us and ever present around us. Harness it and be able to transmute.
Be one with the energy of the cosmos.
Control your own microcosmic orbit.
Control your energy. Prepare it for a long life.
Apply it for the necessary manifestations.

"The first step in working with internal energy is the Microcosmic Orbit Meditation. This meditation trains one to sense, direct, and cultivate more energy. This meditation is the core technique to all other universal TAO practices. The Microcosmic Orbit is the main energy circuit, nourishing all the channels and meridians in the body. Circulating energy within this channel removes blockages and activates more Chi to revitalize the body. Through this practice, one learns to recognize what Chi feels like while moving energy through the Governor meridian (running up the back) and the functional or Conception meridian (coming down the front of the body). The Microcosmic Orbit dramatically increases the quantity of our internal energy."

Good Thoughts

Uncertainty moves in and out of life
Consistent like the ocean's tide
One day comes with a clear path
The next
Clueless
No signs
No sure steps
Head slowly these days
Life is a long journey
Make a stand
A bold movement
A show of life
Self Reassurance

"The only thing that makes life possible
is permanent, intolerable uncertainty:
not knowing what comes next."
-Ursula K Le Guin

42

Insignificance may be a feeling along your path
It's a big world out there after all
Sit with that feeling
Nurture the bond
Of you and your own significance
Your personal worth
You are enough
You matter
In more ways than one
All are apart of the whole
The web of life
The feeling will pass with understanding
Acceptance of the big picture
The play on emotions
Duality is experienced
You are enough
You are worthy
Worthy of life
And All
Its most beautiful experiences

"I will keep telling you that you are important, deserving, loving, intelligent, worthy, compassionate, beautiful, creative, inspiring, brave, true, strong, and able, until you finally realize it for yourself."

What wakes you up
What drives you
What is worth your energy
What feeds your soul
Boosts your spirits
Where does your circulation
Best Flow
Incorporate work, ways of living,
people, and environments that enrich
inrich your life.
Key

"Some of life's best pleasures are simplest ones. Enrich your life with more of them and your heart will be happy." -Robin S Sharma

Knowledge is accessible
You can study, learn, and master
Learning is a lifelong process
Wisdom is gained through experience
Knowledge & Information
Are more easily attainable
Than ever before
Still it is your responsibility
More than ever
To acquire knowledge
To learn and unlearn information
Your brain works like a computer
Give it the necessary knowledge
Add new information to compute
At a higher level
Up to date processing power

"Each one of us has all the wisdom and knowledge we ever need right within us. It is available to us through our intuitive mind, which is our connection with universal intelligence." -Shakti Gawain

Will power
Self propulsion
Aim for the furthest star
Lifetimes away
Set your course amongst legends
Enjoy the ride
With a dream bigger than your own life
Work is simple
A meaningful chip away
Knowing fully one day
Someone else will have to swing
Life, the world, society, continues
Dream astronomical dreams
It doesn't matter where you end up

"I think I've done all that I wanted to do. As long as I can be helpful and keep going. That's the main thing."
–A Centenarian

"Keep right on to the end of the road. That's my motto." –A Centenarian

It won't always move
As fast as you want it to
Life that is
You may see the future
That will soon be the present
Almost smell it, touch it, feel it
Yet still
The dream is still a dream
It may manifest tomorrow
Or the next day

Today you may be man|woman
Tomorrow King|Queen
Be present today
Herein see a gift
Just as abundant
As the dream soon to be

Things start to happen
Momentum begins to build
Wind begins to blow at your back
Universe will show you
You are on the right path
Manifestations materialize
Invisible becomes visible
You will know your Alchemy
Control what you can control
Continue on your path
Signs will point you
In one direction or another
Stay the course until you see them
When it's wrong you will know
Gently or abruptly
When it's right
You will know

In the midst of everything
Come back to stillness
Silence
Re cultivate your energy
Tap back in to the inner you
Life can move fast
Blessings can shower you
Root yourself in that
In that high vibration
In that grateful state of being
Find stillness there
Manage your life energy
Sustain – Maintain – Increase

Abundance is all around
Everpresent
Seen after a perspective shift
Seen through a new lens if you will
Ask yourself now...
What in my life do I have
to be grateful for?
Ask yourself now...
What in my immediate surroundings
can i choose to feel
gratitude for?
Choose to tap into abundance in this
moment no matter the circumstances.
You have just welcomed more abundance
into your future.
Take your eyes off lack
Don't look for things that aren't there
Don't look for what's missing
It will present
Prepare by rooting your vibration
In the feeling of dreams fulfilled

Ask yourself questions
Constructively
Speak to yourself
Empowering
Ask questions to the Universe
Speak to the air
Hear through the wind
Listen for the whispers
that disrupt the silence
How would your problems look...
If they were solved?
Stimulate the mind with this question
Seek positive answers
Then find them

Trust in the
Unseen
Uncertain
& Unfolding

The Universe
The Higher Mind
Will never
Give up
Your attention
Will be
Gotten
Your soul is on a path of continuous
advancement. You will learn the lessons
required of this incarnation.
If not?
They will chase you to the next lifetime.
The next
Incarnation
Don't resist
Persit
On your life path
You agreed to your own forms of
awakening

Life channels through you
Vessel
Receiver
And
Transmitter
Your expressions
What you express
Is your expression of life
Your story and your performance
Let them be gifts
In gratitude to life
In return for life
Giving you the gift to be

Steady yourself
Much life yet to live
No matter your age
Time is an illusion
There is much you will accomplish
Necessary time resource and reward
Provided
Be willing to take deep breaths
Check out
Unplug
Steady yourself
Much life yet to live
Be willing to take deep breaths
Check out
Unplug
Steady yourself
Much life yet to live
Be willing to take deep breaths

Life can consume you
Distract you
Cause you to drift
Don't get caught sleeping
Every day, minute, moment
Is a chance to ascend
Transcend
Live your purpose
Tap into the Cosmos
Feel the vastness of life
& your connectedness to it

Be humbled by your own presence.

It is already done
What is meant to be
Will be
Trust in all things
All life
Is divinely guided
Blessing & Lessons
Sowing & Reaping
The path will appear
Before your foot hits the ground
Not a moment to soon or to late
All has its purpose
All has its reason
All has its teaching
Change is the constant
Don't cling & grasp
Release & Let go
Surrender to the universal way of
things, experience wu-wei.

You will taste your expectations
Like a grain of salt
Sometimes you'll enjoy it
But you already knew how it would taste
Other times you'll expect more, better
Of life & of yourself
You expect dessert
Yet taste salt
You've shot for the stars
Yet haven't left the ground
Now what
Stay woke
Send a declaration to the universe
Here I am
Here I stand
Feed me salt?
I'd rather starve
Keep your aim high
Don't break your standards
Declare & Demand
Your expectations of life
& of yourself

Be Moved
Allow yourself to deeply feel
Life is but a dream
Life is but a journey
Be moved
And move
Take it all in
Absorb the experience
In simple moments of solitude
In connected moments in crowds
Attune to the energetic flow
Life moves
In many ways
Move with it
Be moved by it

Enjoy the Sun
Soak in the rays
Accept the nutrients
Allow the activation
Our bodies respond to light
Feed from it
Are nurtured by it
So go out of your way
When the chances arise
Step into the light
Step into good vibes
Thank you Sun
For your Light
For your Energy

It is ok
To crawl into bed
KNOWING
I will live tomorrow
Better than I lived today

Tunnel vision
Focus
Concentration
Add these attributes to your action

A completed project, is no more
than moments of attentive work,
strung together over a period of time.

Your work will near the finish as you
attend to the steps in front of you.

Do not be discouraged by the mountain
Bite into what you can chew

If you have a key
Seek the lock
If you have the lock
Seek the key

Know what you are looking for.

Appreciate opportunities to grow
Chances to learn
Become more experienced
Gain wisdom
Life is expansive & ever expanding
You are life
Continuously expand yourself
Push your own limits
Seek new horizons
Explore new possibilities
Perform when called upon
Speak when spoken too
Break down barriers
Shatter paradigms
& at all times
Listen
To the words, lessons, advice, of those
around you. Also listen to the lessons taught,
by the way of life, the divine order of things.
All is as it is meant to be.
Understand Wisdom Knowledge
Follow

Don't let
Decisions
Be
Detrimental
"tending to cause harm"
It may take negative repercussions
From your own decisions
For you to see
That inside you
Is the power to foresee...
Don't react
Pause
If the outcome of your decision,
may tend to cause harm...
Don't make it.

Don't be blinded by emotions

Pause
Foresee
Decide
Done

Good Thoughts

You must find

Or seek

Something, anything
No matter how seemingly
Insignificant or significant
To pursue practice preach perform
The seek itself may be the
lifelong journey
Or you may have known since birth

Follow the unfolding
You believe what you see
Otherwise you wouldn't see it

Accept now
Change from here

Enjoy and appreciate
Allow the necessary time & space
To do so adequately
Cherish the meaning you give
To that which you love, care, and feel
Soul Blueprints
Designed by
Hidden by
Found by
Ourselves
The physically manifested
World around you
Matters
Knock...Knock
To you
Co-Created Agreed Experienced
Transcended
Cherish your transcendence

Develop yourself
Create your character
Prepare your presentation
The reflection in the mirror
Is your greatest asset
Your goldmine
What do you see?
What do you want to see?

Do what is needed to become

Emotional reactions
Must be resisted like temptation
When they begin to bubble
Fighting their way to the surface
Breathe
Circulate energy
Rebalance
Much learning can occur
& an opportunity for healing
There may be wounds inside of you
of unconscious origin
Locked and sealed in the depths
of the subconscious mind
Now they've been triggered
Unlocked
Who or what was the key?
What is your treasure that has
been hidden within?

Life may not always feel right
You may not always feel right
That's alright
Life can be a roller coaster
Yet
Humans tend to raise their awareness
In times of hardship
To levels not normally operated at
Take your focus off your pain
Become present of your vastness
In all moments
Use your heightened awareness
Shift it from sickness to healing
From the old to the new
These feelings are gifts of energy
Utilize them
Transmute them

Opportunities will appear
Some subtle
Some a slap in the face
The future of those may be unclear
So too may be the present
One thing can be certain
You will only find what's all in store
After Acceptance

Live
Where
You can
Allow yourself
To live healthy
To enjoy peace of mind
To hear silence
To share in good company
To be you freely
Not fearfully

Sickness is not worth your energy
Worry not worth your thought
Surround yourself
From the inside out
With
Good energy
Good vibes
Good people
Live in
& create a
Positive Environment

Good Thoughts

TEACH
THE
WORLD
HOW
TO
FIND
WHAT
IS
HIDDEN
INSIDE

Starting
With
Yourself
ONE
INDIVIDUAL
AT
A
TIME

Sleep
Rest
Nap
Meditate
Close your eyes
Detach from stimulus
Hear the silence
See the darkness
Relax
Recoup
Rejuvenate
Renew
YOU

Get lost in the stars

Sweet Dreams

What will you become?
Now that all is possible...
Any reality...
What will your intentions be?
Now that both honesty & deception
are available.
How will you see the world?
Knowing peace & chaos exist...
How will you view yourself?
Know compassion or judgment
are your choice...

Utilize your will power
Your decision power
Your emotional control
Your choice of attitude

This life is what you make it
You are who you choose & work to become
Change & fresh starts are constant
So ask & decide

Laugh
Smile
Lighten your load
Release the tension
In your body
Stretch
Reach
Elongate
Break the chains
No longer Rigid
Build your flexibility
Free the body
Free the mind

Everyone has demons
Self created
Or blamed on others
The choice comes down to power
What or who will you allow power over you?
Power over **you**?
Nothing & no one has power over you
Yet everyone gets triggered...
Why?
Moved to tears, laughter, rage...
What causes, triggers,
emotions and reactions.
Is it different for everyone?
Can they be controlled?

Find the source
Heal the wound

Learn something new today...

Welcome to today
Future is uncertain
Presence all we see
In the present moment
Only place to be
Peace can always be
In the present moment
Peace is all we see

You never know what the day will hold
You never know what tomorrow may bring
No need for worry or fearful expectations
Miracles are possible
Live practically to counter fears
Yet expect the beautiful unexpected
There is no need to restrict life
Much is out of our control
Become the rock in happy times & sad
For you are the constant
The Truth
The Continuous
Circumstances & environment will change
Yet you will always be found in the center
Your world revolves around you
Keep it moving flowing evolving

Don't get to far ahead of yourself
All is good All is well
Always in the moment
Dare to dream
Shoot for the stars
Be willing to change
Think Big
Work small
Long time perspective

Don't overestimate
What you can accomplish in a day
Don't underestimate
What you can accomplish
In a week month year decade
Combine
Work, Ethic & Patience

Good Thoughts

You can save one everyday
You can be saved once everyday
Some people come & go
Some people stay for long
In these relationships
Both fleeting & everlasting
You can save one everyday
One will save you each day

Gifts can be given
In many ways
Find time to give them
Everyday
As we give
So it is given
Send out to the universe
What you wish to receive
Give gifts of love
Love you shall see
Sow seeds of abundance
Prosperity Trees

All must spend time alone
Or you might forget who you are
But there is something beautiful
about good company
Sharing time and presence
Never to return
With those you love and care for
Time is passing
Change is constant
People even whom you're closest to
Live & Die
Cherish the presence shared
Thank you for the times I've had
Thank you for the times I'm having
& the times still to come
Spent with the people I love
What a blessing
Hug the ones you love

Sing your song
La la la la la la la la laaa
The point of singing is to sing
The reason for playing is play
Children understand intuitively
They don't justify or judge
They act in the way
Truest to themselves
They act for joy
To enjoy

So enjoy life
Don't justify your happiness
Don't hold yourself back
Pursue joy

Some places
Times
People
Memories
& environments
May return
Ones you like
& ones you don't
This too shall pass
Be with it
Be there
Trust the change
& the beautiful moment
Own it
Accept it
Allow it
Receive the present
Always
Open

Who you fighting???
Who you fighting???
Who you fighting???

Is anything frightening?
Not usually, TV maybe...

Our minds constantly fight...
Imaginary battles
Over & over again

Deep breath in
Sip of water
All is good All is well
A new day
Free of past spells
We are not fighting
We are free
Peace is here. Peace is now.

Good Thoughts

Enjoy yourself
Your company
Your time
Entertain yourself
Laugh & cry alone
Move yourself
& get out of the way
Give yourself necessary attention
Don't forget the details
Take care of you
Maybe you'll be privileged
to take care of others
Love you
Maybe you'll be blessed
with others to love
Enjoy you
Maybe you'll be surrounded
by beautiful souls to enjoy
Treat yourself
as you wish to be treated

Get back on track
Whenever you derail
Pick yourself right back up
Anytime you fall
Continue forward
The journey never ends
The track never runs out
Continue forward
Onward with life
Onward with living
Onward with thriving, surviving
Onward with achieving, progressing
Onward with growth health healing
Onward with life
Don't you stop

Signs of the times
You'll learn to see what is
coming & going
Living & Dying
You'll stop hiding the truth
From your own eyes
See clearly now
Reinvent when necessary
Re create where needed
Life is that malleable
Daily disciplined work
Is success
Succeed every day
In your own way
Following your own heart

Seek firsts
Experience is worth more than money
Priceless moments
Priceless knowledge
Welcomes wisdom
New growth
New rewards
New standards

On the other side
Of your comfort zone

Transcend the energy
Utilize nerves & excitement
Harness it
New Level

What to do
When you don't know
What to do

Clean the world around you
Stir up the energy in your home
Clean you
Warm cleansing salt bath
Take care of yourself
& the blessings around you

Shows the Universe you are
grateful for all that
has happened
and is happening

 Also ready for new to come

Some days don't feel right
Move with them anyways
There must always be a reason
Find the answer
Transcend the circumstance
Find the vibration
Transcend the state of being
Life is constantly changing seasons
Constant tides of emotion & energy
Extract the good
From each & all moments

Slowest goings are always at the start
Momentum is always hardest to gain
From the beginning
The hardest part is starting new motion
Redirecting your work focus
energy intent
Redirecting whenever &
where necessary in life
Allow the required time
Needed to gain momentum
To build energy, to create a process
To form new habits, sow new seeds
Reap new rewards
Allow the process
Lay the bricks
Do what is required
Let the future unfold
Play your role

I feel the sunshine
Feels how I feel
Radiant
Multi Dimensional
Everpresent
Every where & no where
All at once
This life experience
Is an energy ride
You are the energy
I am my energy
My life force
I shall apply it
Toward manifestation & creation
that make the world
a better brighter place
Paint your picture...
of an impactful life for yourself
Then live it.

Continue to re-program
Reach your subconscious
Your children's children will thank you
Rewire your supercomputer
Improve & attend to your body & mind
Your genes though only a foundation
Have been and will be passed on
They have been and will continue to be
Altered by you
Upgrade your genetics
Epigenetics
Above
Genetics

The world is both
Massive & small
You can lay down
Close your eyes
Feel it all
Looking out your window
However vast you can see
Still only a glimpse
Of Earth & Humanity
Get in touch with
The world that resides
Within you
Get in touch with
The world that is
Both you & larger than you...

Dream the largest
Dream you can dream
Build the biggest building you can build
Fight the greatest fight you can fight
Leave a great legacy worth living
Yes worth living
Allow ideas & goals
For a brighter future
Fuel your today
Embrace tomorrow
The idea that life goes on...
Simple as that...
Live today work today dream today
Love today
Be driven by tomorrow
What does your tomorrow look like?
What do you want it to look like?
Create for tomorrow
Today

Give for the sake of giving
Love for the sake of loving
Sing for the sake of singing
Play for the sake of playing
Do because you desire to...
Live free
Express
Enjoy
None other than yourself can stop you

Don't worry for tomorrow
All is well today
No troubled thoughts of what
may show
False
Evidence
Appearing
Real
Day Terrors
The unspoken mental chatter
Full of what could go wrong
Make peace with the infinite
For of course...yes
All possibilities are possible
Only now moment is real
Root your future
Your uncertainties
In present presence

Disappointments may occur
Maybe even from yourself
Lay your head down to rest
Go through the motions tomorrow
Energy will re-balance eventually
Hold your head up
Hold your head up.

1 0 1

Trust the process below your feet
The world works in much
More different ways then
You think
Don't you think?
The world works in ways before mind
and time.
Something birthed life
What birthed something
Some chicken and the egg
Really though
What you believe matters
What you perceive
ALters ReaLity
Trust what you see
ALter what you perceive
Alters what you see

Good Thoughts

Life is like a race
More marathon than sprint
Yet in each race there comes a time
When we must pick up the pace

Where can you work harder?
Give more effort?
Be more productive?

You know, now apply.

Daily actions
Daily habits
Can be either creative or destructive
Discipline your daily regimen
Make every day count
Plan the necessities
Make room for growth
For success
For advancement
Create routines & programs
that work for you
Routine to kickstart your morning
Routine for work health life
Even still
Always flexible & adaptive

Focus Focus
Not Hocus Pocus
Imprint your intentions
Life can do nothing
Other than agree and conform
You truly have the power
Are you using it?
We cannot control everything
Much of the world is beyond our grasp
But we can control & rule
over ourselves
& that is enough

Create Creator

Lost & Finding
A clear step I hope to take
Where to go
Oh where will I go
I am willing
I am able
Standing stagnate in the fog
Vision blinded
Stay standing
Never fall
One day I wish to see
Where the next step is meant for me

Turn the page
Stop rereading if you wish to write
The future is not found in the past
Past has led to present
Present leads to future
Unaffected by past
So Go Forth
All who feel called upon
Strive for anew
Live more chapters

Turn your pages
Faster than the ink dries

I don't need to be there
I am always where I need to be
Now if there is a there I wish to be
I must first solve the riddle
Of being here
Here is not there
Here is a necessary route
On way to there
Enjoy the ride

Do not resist your expansion
It only hurts
When you fight to hold on
Let Go
Release
Trust Fall
Universe will catch you

Learn the lessons of this day
Everyday
Give Thanks

Exercise
Mind
Body
Soul
Nourish Yourself
Allow healing recuperation
& breakdown
Build yourself up
Utilize discipline to construct habits
To create routines in your days that
Develop the ideal you
You are both rock & sculptor
Chisel away bit by bit
Piece by piece
Day by day
Witness the divine revealing
Every step of the way

Where or where have I lost my fear
Seemed to have dropped it
Blew away in thin air
Followed & followed the scent I tried
Thinking fear was a key
For something inside
Now I love fear
I leave it alone
If it comes to my door
I welcome it home

"Invite Mara to tea..."

"Out beyond ideas of wrong doings &
right doings there is a field...
I'll meet you there." –Rumi

No need for judgment
See through open eyes
Not filters
See with eyes wishing to understand
Not thinking they already do
We have much to learn at all times
From all people
And all situations
Live to learn understand heal
& appreciate

Thank You

Live in a glass house
We all need and deserve privacy
Those who can be themselves
At all times
In all places
Live the most comfortable
Loosen up
Let go
Let the world see the real you
Let you
see
the real
you

The day is long
Much can be accomplished
Give it your best shot
Knowing most of the time
You get a fresh start
Welcome to the morning
The start of anew
Unfathomable Number
Of new possible realities
Soon to come
Eagerly awaiting
For you to live your day
Where will you go
What will you do
When all outcomes are possible
Each & every new morning
The future is at your fingertips

Transcend Transcend
Like the butterfly flies
The cocoon you're in

Is juSt

A staTe

Of mInd

Today oh day
How you've flown away
I thank you for the time
Shared my way
I hope I used it well
My intentions are good
When I arise
I do my best
I believe I try
To live a life
Worth living
Before
I, dies.

Trust your restrictions
& your freedoms
Conservative when necessary
Reckless when allowable
Play with duality
Understand its simple
Light switch nature
You are still the flipper
The controller of the switch
Give yourself boundaries
To unleash *you're* Energy
Room to spread your wings
Unhindered by limitations
Dancing with the shadow

1 1 8

Life
Moves & Flows
Twists & Turns
Allowing the journey
To
Keep going
Participate in movement
Take action
In the direction
Of your goals & desires
Energy is constantly moving
Guide your own
Go your own way
The speed & direction
Of your decision & choosing
Free to roam
Free to stay in a lane
Free to be
Freely Live

You musn't always be in a rush
Time can be slow
When you look at it that way
Don't worry on
when you will accomplish
Do the work, walk the path
That will lead to your goals eventually
You will get there
The mind only chatters during in action
A chance to sneak thoughts in
Go out & do
Take action toward your dreams
Doors will open
Walls will crumble
You will become
& continue
Becoming

Hammer chisel think
Hammer chisel think
Hammer chisel think
Hammer chisel think
Hammer chisel think
Hammer chisel think
Hammer chisel think
Hammer chisel think

Hammer chisel hit
Hammer chisel hit
Hammer chisel hit
Hammer chisel hit
Hammer chisel hit
Hammer chisel hit
Hammer chisel hit
Hammer chisel hit
Hammer chisel hit
Hammer chisel hit
Hammer chisel hit

1 2 1

Warm rays on a cold day
Sunshine blue skies chilled
Clarity cuts through
Pause
Download
Now onto the next move
More intelligent
More disciplined
More informed
More speed
More endurance
More technique
More sustainable
Move Forward
Life will slow you down
& speed you up
Receive the download
Refuel Reset Recharge
Now empty yourself...again

Constantly
Radiate Healing Cleansing
Loving Vibrations
In all places
In all moments
Be the beacon of peace
Your calming vibes
Will soothe all around
The heartfield is unseen
Not unfelt
We are all affected
We are all effecting

Cultivate Positive Effects

It will transform you
& all those around you

1 2 3

Perspectives need shifting
Negative filters need removing
Clear vision
Future unjudged
Acceptance of what is
Balanced
Action toward what could be
Whatever you see inside
Your mind's eye
Your pineal gland
Your visions & dreams
They are right for you
They are real for you
Or they would not be
Hear your truths
See your life
Follow your path
You know where to go
What to do
When you
...silence your mind
Hear your heart
She speaks, calls, and cries out
Always to you
With Love

Good Thoughts

Do you believe that anything is possible?
Then believe in the best outcomes always
Believe in lifetime growth
Believe that this too shall pass
Believe that no matter the situation
No matter the circumstance
If there is breath in your body
You have a chance
You don't know how long it will last
In this moment
In that moment
You have a chance
A chance to change
To reinvent
To blossom
To continuously become
Say yes to the opportunity
Fight on if you can stand
Say yes to relationship
Move forward amidst adversity
Don't stop
Ever change
Ever become
Forever Transcend
As long as you can stand
Push forward
Strike back
Defend & Live
Offensively strike
Without being struck

Good Thoughts

1 2 5

Sometimes I just don't know what to do.
Who to be. Where to go.
What song to sing.
Life offers windows of clarity.
Fleeting glimpses seen only for a moment
Vision of a path
Hope for a continuous road ahead
Take it for what it is
A glimpse of a possible future
If the directions feel right
GO
If not
Wait
Patience
The right feelings will come
Nurture yourself at all times
Help the body heal the body
Mind will follow
If you wait to long though
Weight may follow
Causing dis-ease
Not at ease
Of the heart

You cannot ignore
Your heart forever
It calls out to you constantly
And will eventually have your full attention

Peace
Love
Positivity
Health
Wealth
Happiness
Peace
Love
Positivity
Health
Wealth
Happiness
Peace
Love
Positivity
Health
Wealth
Happiness
Peace
Love
I Love You

Good Thoughts

1 2 7

It's hard sometimes
To know where to go
Even in an infinite world
Where all is possible
Limits are only perception
Nothing can stop you
Except you
And it's not even stopping yourself
It's not starting

Waiting for clarity
So what to do
When you know & believe
Everything is attainable
Where to take the first step

Don't move
Not yet

Let your energy settle to
The flow of the universe
The one song of life
Sit still silent listen
Grounded rooted in the now moment
Place your hand on your heart
Speak to it
Who am I? What does my heart desire?
What path leads to my highest version of myself?
What opportunities are available & which shall I choose?
How to best live, grow, & become?
Feel your heart
Feel the answers
To all your questions...

Good Thoughts

1 2 8

There's much more to see
Than meets the eye
Eye is a tool
We see with the mind
So close your eyes
See the world inside
Open again
See only a projection
Maybe even reflection
Pay attention to it all
Mind the details
The gold of the mine|mind
All is teaching
All is healing
All is flowing
Move with the world you see
Love the world you see
Improve the world you see
You are your world you see

1 2 9

There seems to be a spirit, an energy
That flows to and through
Swim with it and catch the wave
Develop your balance
Harness energy from the world
Outside your body
The interconnected web of life
You'll know when you're in sync
Or that you've always been in touch
With the abundant life of giving
Universe
Energy that always
Has been will be is you
Life is Life
Apart of the whole is the whole
Unified on Cosmic scale
No self
Just life
Life everlasting

Play your role
Sing your song
Dance your dance
Do your work
Be yourself
You I we all
Keep the world turning
Keep life existing
Keep life living

Live for the benefit of all life

Good Thoughts

130

Walk your path forward
Into the new
Leave behind that which no longer
Fits the new you
You can only be hold carry so much
Let go shed old skins
Form new identities
Analyze what is and is not working in your life
Analyze your old & new standards of success
Realize that which no longer suits you
Re tailor your life
Jump Levels
Stretch Reach Grow
Detox be feel eat light
Your bodies been asking for it...eat conscious
Change the details in the portrait of your life
Watch a beautiful new image blossom

It is never too late to do something now...
With what you have, where you are at, be grateful, and ask...

What can I do here now, to better my life, life around me,
and all life for the uncertain future?

I can only control what I can control
I must let the rest go
I trust the Universe knows
I trust the path that is shown
Thank You

Good Thoughts

Say yes to life and see
What appears and disappears
Let go of the old
Embrace the new
Jump
Dare to fly
Allow the breeze to catch you
Carry you
Into the sky
Mold reshape change as you go
One can always adjust with momentum in tow
It is always hard to push the rock
When starting out slow
Do what you must
From where you are at
Reach above
For a helping hand
Then send one down
As soon as you can
Give Receive Work Sow Reap
This life is a process
Not to be beat
A game to play
Not one to be won
Enjoyed Loved Lived
What blessing we've been given...
What blessings will we give...

Good Thoughts

Life will offer new
Stay up to speed
Life will increase
Move forward
Scenery will change
Keep Walking
Earth is still & moving
So shall we be
Still & Moving
Open eye meditation
See interpret asses act
No reaction pause space
This world has enough space for all
Time won't pass you by
Journey Journey
Carry On
Learn through living
Hear your song
Follow your heart
The pull is strong
Like strings of thread they nudge and guide,
the puppet master of a subconscious mind.
The brain is born into the world in a receptieve accepting
hypnotic state, then programed by all we see hear smell
taste touch, all influenced by the world around us. As we
grow mature self awaken, our brain waves change, old
thoughts, old beliefs are no longer a match to the
new vibrations new frequencies.
Allow what no longer aligns to fall away.

Good Thoughts

133

Send the occasional smoke signal to the sky
Let the universe know you're still here
Let the smoke cleanse the energy around you
Let the flames massage your mind
Control of fire may very well have been the first
psychedelic transcendence in the minds of humans.
While staring into the flames our ancestor's minds may
have relaxed into a meditative state beyond fight or flight.
Beyond survival.
Allowing enough space for intuition to strike.
Possibly shifting perspectives from surviving to thriving.
Light your fire. Let the flames burn thought away.
Quiet your mind
We are thriving here
Live above survival
Choose to aim for higher ideals
Love Compassion Humanity
Whatever it is for you
Live larger than yourself
Then so shall your impact be
Shifts in thought set a new sail
A new direction guided by a clear mind
Guided by abundance
Guided by limitless possibility
Let fire burn away what led you here
New intuition now seen clear.
Where we are now in the moment
is where we are supposed to be.
Where we are going is up to us &
determined by what we believe.

Good Thoughts

134

Monitor yourself
Don't let the leash to long on bad habits
We choose to do that which we do
Consciously or un
So set yourself up for success
Position yourself for luck & opportunity
"Fortune favors the bold…"
Gain daily momentum
Progression leads to results
Progression encourages happiness hope & energy
Keep moving
Keep trying
Keep seeking
Keep finding
"The dots will seem connected when looking backward…"
until then
Dance your dance in the face of uncertainty
In the midst of constant change
Evolve grow flow along
Your energy too will continue on

BE STILL BE NOW
BE PRESENT FOREVER
ALL HAPPENS HERE
ALL HAPPENS ALWAYS NOW

Harness yourself in the moment, each and every now
moment, win the moment, again & again, win the days,
win the months, win the years, win life.

Good Thoughts

1 3 5

Do what is necessary to heal you, to help you,
love you, care for you, support yourself.
You are both a resource & resourceful.
Tend to yourself
You are your greatest asset
Be honest be real when looking and speaking with
the one in the mirror. Peel layers of filters revealing
the raw you. Love what you see.
Daydream on what you can become.
How you can reshape you mold you evolve you
There is Levels to this
New Levels in energy Light Love
New Levels in passion purpose drive
New Levels of conscious awareness
Play above keep climbing striving

You and your Life know no Limits
See what you find
Above the horizon

Day by day
Future & present change
Day by day
Past fades away
Rewritten by the moment
Replaced by the next
All in congruence All intertwined
Both dark & light Both reason & rhyme
Can you tell time?
Can you even lie?
How far will you dive into the darkside
Only the absence of light you may say
I say you are the light avoiding the dark
Shine your awareness
Give its needed attention
By doing so
You are the light in the dark
Thus darkness fades
No more absence

1 3 7

Some days feel like bumps in the road
All precious all life all living all learning
Transmute the feelings of hard days
Understand the root cause
Allow the emotions to release
To be felt experienced freed
Then utilized
Find your strength in overcoming
Yourself your bad habits your weaknesses
Conquer & create you
Daily carve the statue
Daily grow the mind
Daily nurture the body
Some days are hard
What you have is what you have
Where you are is where you are
What you've done has been done
What is past is gone
What is future unwritten
Take up your pen
Write the story of your life
As a conscious creator
Direct yourself where you go
Wish to go
All is possible in the now
For the future
Destiny infinite maybe uncertain
Maybe unclaimed
Declare your life
Choose its direction

Good Thoughts

138

Patience & Action
Plan your forward progress
Plan the work
Work the plan
Day by day step by step
Choose to take pre meditated action
Thoughts & plans are ideas until your
Action brings them life
Act in the world
On dreams & goals inspired by your mind
Make physical your visions of what's possible
Act even for the reason of no regret
If you wish too...you owe yourself to try
Give this life all you've got, it already gave all to you
Don't let inaction hold you back
Find out what is possible for you
Test the waters make your moves
Life will aid in your motion
You will blaze your own trails
You will find your way in the sea
Life is large vast...wander it
Explore adventures seek & find
Be not limited by fears of your mind

It's true that we don't know how the future turns out.
If we act though, we may push in a direction we wish to go,
we may attract people opportunities miracles, by being in
the right place right state at the divine right time...

Good Thoughts

139

Healthy Release
The mind will twist & toil at times
Let it alone
Enter the body
Run jump sweat punch kick stretch swim
Movement releases tension
It may take a marathon
But the mind will quiet
Freed by the body
At times too body shall speak
Listen to it's aches & pains
Recognize them, nurture healing
Care to the trapped emotions
When needed
Leave the body
Take silent trips of meditation
Journey into the moment the ever presence
Knowing your true being is
Interconnected to all energy
All life and it all flows to and through you
The answers we seek
The healing we need
It was will always be
Inside of us
Available to be found
Available to be tapped into

Good Thoughts

Reconnect with the sound of nature
The essence of life
The pace of life may seem to
pick up and may seem to slow
Underneath those surface waves
moves a constant flow
Life always moves at the same speed
Our perception of momentum changes
Don't get too caught up and easily distracted
Take the time to close your eyes
To retreat from stimuli
Reconnect with your own energy
You are your own fuel
Your ever burning flame
Tap into your life energy
What moves motivates uplifts & inspires you
Go in that direction
You'll guide yourself
On life's journey by following your pull
& navigating your push
Trust in what calls out to you
What pulls on your heartstrings
Also trust in what you push away
And be strong in your push
Remove yourself from where you
don't belong, to find your
way to where you do

A life of "leela"
A life of play
A life of dance
A childlike playful way of living
Choose to interact with the world
In a calm loving manner
No rush no worry no push no shove
Navigate & guide your ship
Don't fight the current
Mold your present manifestation
Make conscious choices
Sow seeds for the harvest your heart desires
There is always a level of trust & patience
A time of belief & vision
Before you reap
Before you see the fruits
Keep planting all the while knowing
How delicious the future will taste
Plant you must don't stare at the field
Power lives in every seed
Only to grow when set free
Give yourself the chance to grow
The increase of luck
The opportunity to succeed
Use your attention and energy to the work that leads to your
dreams goals desires purpose. Follow the path, trust the
journey. See what happens after you take the first step...the
second step...the third step...the...

1 4 2

Why? is a delicate question
Requires delicate intimate answers
Be careful in your demands of why
directed toward others
toward their way of being
Why is a question that must be asked
Brought up reflected on...gently
Truly first we must be able to
do this kindly with ourselves
In finding our roots in the
Unknown or uncertain
We face our own truths
Ask we seek we find
Our demand to know why of others
Must then be seen as a mirror
As a coping technique to not demand
The answer or direct the question
To ourselves
Be cautious in this world of mirrors
The "Golden Rule" is always in play
They are all apart of you
& you apart of them
Love all aspects of yourself
Seek the understanding
In yourself
From yourself
Ask you why? Ask you who? Ask you what?
Ask of yourself to grow learn unlearn relearn
Ask of yourself to change evolve love transcend

Good Thoughts

1 4 3

Somehow hold steady
In the face of any & every adversarie
In the face of any & all situations
Laugh don't believe it
The mirror will be forced to shatter
No one outside you constructs your world
Trust in change
What do you have to lose?
I mean truly life is a gift from the start...
It always keeps giving...
Exactly what you ask believe act for
Yes, there are recipes to manifestation
You are the baker, you have the ingredients
To create anything
Choose the dish
Follow the recipe
Use your ingredients

Re Direct Reality
When you have a dream
When you're told you can't
When you're knocked down
When presented a challenge
Conjure your energy focus thought toward solutions,
on opportunities, fueled with belief & hope, know that
new is possible, that new is now, make changes where
necessary, fight back for the life you want deserve &
are destined to live.

Good Thoughts

1 4 4

Something has to work out
Change is constant
Keep hope
At all times
Through all things
Life changes
"This too shall pass"
Always law
In good times & bad
Hindsight is 20/20
Enjoy trust learn in the moment
All life always now
Here leads to there
There will become here
The future will eventually become now
Your world will be as you dream
Explore the path while you're on it
Take in the sights smells sounds
Notice the magic
Believe in what is not yet seen

Good Thoughts

1 4 5

All is well now & always
The contrast may try to say otherwise
Create in the face of
Love the mirror...Whatever it shows
A chance to heal...As soon as we know
Where we come from...Helps us where we go
What a beautiful journey we have ahead
Off to the stars to make a new bed
Here we lay upon the Earth
A planet of life continued rebirth
Find balance in him find balance in her
Life is ever giving ever growing ever living
The dream continues in all ways
You've lived then
You've lived then
Lived & Live Now
& will continue to live on
In the future Trust in your divine nature
No reason to judge you are alive
You are life as worthy as the most high
Made of stardust same nature as the sky
Connected to all witness your own divinity
All beings all life all in front of your eyes
A reflection of you a reflection of all life
Be loving awareness while witnessing the mirror

Good Thoughts

1 4 6

Feelings Precede Manifestation
Better you feel Better you look
Better you feel Better your world looks
So take time for you
Practice meditation exercise eat well
Truly though live meditative
Calm your state of being constantly
Breathe deep Breathe gratitude
Keep mantras in your mind at all times
Thank You Thank You Thank You
If all you think is thank you
All you see is blessings
Thank You Thank You Thank You
Peace Love Positivity Health Wealth Happiness
I Love You I Love I Love I Love
I love you
I am sorry
Please forgive me
Thank you
I love you
I am sorry
Please forgive me
Thank you
Thank you

Good Thoughts

Right Place Right Time
Always
I AM THAT I AM
Warrior in the garden
Pass the fighting spirit on
How you do anything
Is how you do everything
Do your best with what you've got
Where you are at
Continually be blessed in the present
Stay current with the flow
The universal rhythm & dance
Choose to move
Decide based on the best you know
Trust the intuition your body shows
Life has reasons that abide in the unseen
You wouldn't be...If you weren't meant to be
Have faith in you & all you see
Travel along your life path
Find a way you'd be honored to give back
Co-create the world you wish too
No limits to what you can be
Surpass the sky with your dreams
Peace Love Positivity
I wish to you and all beings

Good Thoughts

Success is continual progression
A habit
A movement forward
No matter how slight
In the direction of your desire
Of a worthy goal
Toward a self purpose
A knowing
A faith
A belief & trust in self
A state of being
Open receptive allowing
Vibrating Positive
Good energy emitting
Steady long term
Life commitment growth
Always expanding being
Success is much more than the thoughts we think
Don't trick the mind to feel out of sync
Feel Good Feel Feel Good
From within
Feel worthy
You have always been
A gift A child
Life birthed of the stars

Good Thoughts

1 4 9

Seek find cultivate create
Your own medicines
Your own food
The land of the Earth offers
Healing & Nourishment
Relish in the abundance of what you need
Moderate unnecessary excess
Balance shows discipline
Creates harmony
Internal flow
Though you must be your best caretaker
You are your biggest responsibility
Take good care of you
Good radiates from you
Then you're seen in a new light
Your being is a miracle maker
You are a miracle co-creator
Walk humble
Do good
Spread love
Positivity is contagious
From where you sit still in meditation
Your heart touches the world
Start here, start now
Hammer chisel life
Start here, start now
Hammer chisel life

Good Thoughts

Stay Up
Stay Ready
Stay Calm
Be Prepared
Universal forces are at play
Day by day by day
In every & all moments of our lives
The power of all life is present
Each breath as meaningful as the one before &
the one to follow
Give importance to yourself
Self worthy
Nothing can diminish the miracle that you are
Close your eyes
Let your energy spread
There is no boundaries between you & the world
Expand your awareness into all of it
Who is the sensor behind the senses
I AM
I Am the hearer
I Am the seer
I Am the taster
I Am the toucher
I Am the smeller
Don't mistake the world & the observer
Settle behind it all
The being the presence the witness
The liver of life
"In the world but not of it"

Good Thoughts

1 5 1

Experiment with life in times of uncertainty
Allow new beginnings just to see what works out
Un attached ambition
Trust the process, enjoy the results
Reap rewards all along the path
Life gets better as we keep living learning loving
More to cherish, more to be grateful for
We are the witnesses of future becoming present
Meaning there is time to influence & co-create
That future
Use your focus
Your attention
Your creative capacities
To first imagine, to visualize
The world you wish to inhabit
& who you wish to be in it
When that vision is clear
Walk the steps toward its manifestation
Realizing you are creating the path as well
Enjoy your self-created growth process
You are strengthening yourself
Molding your highest state of being
View with wonder your continued blossoming

1 5 2

Keep Making Attempts
Keep trying new
Seek New Desires New Passions
Don't be afraid to fall in love again
Don't fear treading a new path again & again & again
Walk where your heart pulls you
Witness the beauty of your travels
No matter near or far go where you feel you must
Never needing to look back wondering what if
Try & Try Again & Again
Constant Reinvention
Constant New Direction
Going where you float
Where it feels like the right place right time
Know you belong
As the world grows so do you
Don't get stuck in the past
Evolve with life change with the times
Be observer & participant of all life has to offer
Be willing to learn & unlearn
To allow new beliefs about what is
foundationally possible
Building anew from the ground up if need be
Never considering defeat valiant in living
Trusting as doors close new entries will open
Always living loving learning pursuing
Choose to find new interests
Adapt & Realign
All is well...All is well
All will happen...On divine time

Good Thoughts

153

Not everyday but on occasion
Doors of change will open
You will be asked to step inside
Physical changes will take place
Your outer mirror will reflect anew
Your being and your environment
will rise to a new vibration
Truly trust this though...
The shift already occured
before you stepped inside.
Whether in mind, heart, soul,
something new was believed.
You knew it was possible before it happened.
"I can not believe it" yes you can or you would not
witness the manifestation...
Parts of yourself may have been accepted
Shadow sides reintegrated
Have faith in your strength & will power
Be ok with surprising yourself
It may take time and toil of the mind to reach a
decision, to make a realization, to see from a new
perspective, to trust your guidance, to feel conviction,
to believe in new possibilities, to love uncertainty.
Once confident clear knowing it is already done
Walk your path in total surrender
Some days will look the same
Some will have doorways

Good Thoughts

1 5 4

Shakily we seek balance as we sit idle
Momentum keeps us centered
Add a little balance to your step
Call the energy up from within
Trust all is well & working out
Now receive the present
Now receive the present
Now receive the present
Now receive the present
Now receive the present
Now receive the present
Now receive the present
All is well & working out
Now receive the present
Thank you for the unfolding
Thank you for the witnessing
Thank you for clarity
Thank you for understanding
Thank you for abundance
Thank you for food energy water shelter
Thank you for health
Thank you for healing
Thank you for health
Thank you for healing
Positive words
Positive vibes
Positive lives radiate
You are loved by loving people
Who will never know your name

Good Thoughts

155

Every breath is beautiful
Life giving
Reaffirming
Reassuring
Thank you for constant reappearance
The present is such a gift
Create meaning for the blessing
You are here You are now
Make the most of it
Day to day living is our stairway to Heaven
Do your best where you are day in and day out
The scenery starts to change
Be grateful for continued experience
Continued breath
Continuing life
The Earth & Stars offer much to delight in
Stick around for a while
Learn to love growth
Observe humanity's evolution
Witness personal changes
Go with the flow
Dip your toes in the ever changing
Ever adapting society & species that we are
There is a call for
Those who hear to be
Radiator of a good vibe sphere
Think good thoughts, speak good words, continuously,
repetitively, constantly, you then offer positive influence to
the world around you.

Good Thoughts

1 5 6

Movement releases tension
Mantras release vibrations
Laughter releases dis-ease
Smile releases compassion
Bow releases pride
Hands release love
Heart releases kindness
Belly releases intuition
Brain releases intelligence
Use the gifts bestowed by body mind energy spirit
Become an Alchemist of energy & emotion
Give Receive Transmit Transmute Transcend
Open yourself to new energies & frequencies
New rate of occurrence
Release internally to experience externally
Don't guard yourself don't hide inside
Your world is lonely that's ok
No matter how many or few surround
In the internal world there is one
Be with the one Be the one
All can be felt here, the sanctuary of inner experience
Handle work out release the tensions & problems of your
life here, take the outer issues inward,
heal the source of the wound.
Let the newfound flow of healing move through, rush,
spread to all areas of body & psyche...then radiate outward
wounded healer...send light love health & healing...
light love health healing...light love health healing...
Send Light Love Health Healing
Send Light Love Health Healing

Good Thoughts

1 5 7

Integrate more love
In all aspects of daily life
Especially mind
Think loving thoughts
Consciously think love
Consciously send love
Consciously act love
Consciously be love
Be the positive loving wave of transformation
Show the world
Show yourself
Give time intention action
To create the world you wish to see
From the world in which you are
Now Living
You are abundance You are abundant
You are a resource You are resourceful
Meaning you have what you need
To get where you are going
Grow from here give love here be love here transcend here
New vibrations take here to a new level
Love Love Love Love
Constantly make peace
Actively creating from the present
For a better now and future
Enjoy and align with yourself
Act in ways that feel fulfilling
Act in ways that feel compassionate
Act in ways that feel healing
Act in ways that feel loving

Good Thoughts

1 5 8

Thank you for now and for always
Gratefulness of presence leads to gracefulness
Life is a beautiful dance a constant flow
Find something to enjoy now, trust the moment
Trust peace in the moment forever love
Trust positive vibration, trust new beginnings
Life is never over while you're alive
Don't stop living...
Death is something, handle it then.

Transcend it then
Accept it now
Live now
Die later

Keep on going...keep on keeping on...
Keep waking up and bringing energy to the day.
Creating a masterpiece of a life well lived.
There are so many different phases of life,
never fear the one you're in.
Trust expansion...Trust growth...
With love enter the unknown
Witness the flowering of life
Act when inspired to move
Act when you see a chance
Play your play...sing your song...dance your dance...
Trust yourself...trust being...
Feel your worth...feel *you're* radiance...
Shining as bright as the stars
All life effects All life
Send peace love positivity in all moments

Good Thoughts

Each day is different offers new
New opportunities, new energy, new unfolding
Truly go with the flow
Enjoy & create strong habits
Be flexible to all the day offers
Life is only stagnant when you are
Life is the same only when looking for similarities
Open up to new experiences
Stay closed to what you don't want
Be brave open up & receive what you need
Don't stop your desires before they manifest
Don't resist expansive energy within
Let yourself blossom become transform
There is limitless flow of energy waiting for you to tap it.
Asking you to reach for it, grasp it, harness it.
The world has your desire...if not...you can create it.
Think ideas that energize. Think thoughts that uplift.
Speak peaceful words. Speak words that create.
Act harmoniously...
Act for & from well being.
Build a good life with
good thoughts good words good actions.
Build a great life with
great thoughts great words great actions
Build a life full of wonder with
wonderful thoughts wonderful words wonderful actions
What life is wonderful to you?
Live full of what you desire to be...
and be.

160

Release into the moment
Walk around in a free body...Let go...Drop all the weight
No tension within...Openflow...Open circulation
Deep breaths...Rejuvenating
Life empties to makes space...Refills...Fulfilling
Tap in to the energy of the day
Tap in to the energy of the now
Feel your interconnectedness to the moment
In the now moment is all life
All happened in previous now
All will happen in a future present now
All is now happening
Accept uncertainty in and of now
Trust is positivity arising from the unknown
Allow & be open to all possibilities
Believe and hold faith in good outcomes
Become magnetized to solutions
Allow influx, everflowing abundance, open for "satori"
Live graceful, in gratitude of "kensho"
You are awakening, You are becoming
You are transcending, You are evolving
All is good & well with the Cosmos
The Divine Order of life...
Or the Divine "leela" play of non order...
Either way is Divinely unfolding
So Trust in...Have Hope in...

Live for...

Bring love into out of now always
Spread good vibes always in from the now moment

Good Thoughts

1 6 1

Find release...Find ease...
Receive...Allow...Life is giving you what you ask...
What are you speaking?
Hear your own words.
Speak a bright future into existence...
Release your action into inspired building...
Inspired experiences...Inspired moments...
Inspired living...Feel your heartbeat...
Hear its desires...What makes your heart pump...
What brings life to your living...
Allow yourself to be invigorated
Let your energy flow free and open
Non restrictive...Tension released
Let life in...Let life through
YOU are the witness of your manifestation
Look out through wonderful eyes
View a wonderful world
The universe wishes your dreams manifest
The imagination is not meant to stay in the mind's eye
Project what you wish to see
Speak Act Observe Create Co-Creator
Test and see the world works with you
Never against you
This incarnation is a process
Ever present being...Ever present becoming
Embrace all stages all speeds all nows
Life happens...You are happening
Let yourself happen & Enjoy your happening
Let yourself be & Enjoy your being

Good Thoughts

Trust your artistic nature
All are creative...no one the less
Follow your daydreams
Down the rabbit hole
Close your eyes...first decide...before you even reopen
See in vivid detail the world your wishes wish you to inhabit
Your healthiest happiest you...
Know the world...begin to live it
Implement what you can in the moment
See what is already here...Know what is on the way
Prepare your receptive mode
Let good feelings flood your body
Magnetize your attraction
Conscious positive focus
Connects your dreams & desires to your day to days
Chin up...Beauty is in the eye of the beholder
The universe is prepared for you to fly
Prep for your take off
Release unnecessary weight
Initiate forward momentum
Find your passion...then follow it...go for it
What would you be happy to do everyday?
If death was soon to be what would you leave behind?
What message do you have for the world?
Life happens in stages
Open innocent bliss
Living your life
Finding you're...reason reasons passion meaning
Daily creating

1 6 3

Start today in a new way
No routine yesterday
Same day everyday
Gone...thrown out the window today
Move different right away
Make your blood flow
Dance your dance...loosen up
Feel Free within your physical
Make the day different
Enjoy nature somewhere else today
Enjoy thinking something else today
In all ways make today a new day
Shine brighter illuminate
Light up Heaven on Earth Light up Heaven at Home
A day away from fear A day away away from worry
A day of relaxed comfortable in your skin being
A day of understanding life goes on
A day of broad horizons, numerous opportunity
A day of peace of mind a day of quiet time
A day of people, A day of place,
A day of good vibrations
Let the day happen, go with it, go where you wish it,
then let it go, let it be, when the nighttime arrives.
Give your best in the light, rest in the night.
On occasion maybe even tonight,
stay up late, enjoy the dark, the still, the silent...
The now, the day, the week, the month, the year...
All have so much to offer, so much to be, so much to see.
Enjoy the day, everyday, enjoy the moment.
Always now, Embrace living, Live grateful.

Good Thoughts

164

Relax the muscle that is your eyes
They are a powerful tool for gathering data
but the brain computes insight
We see with the mind not the eyes
Truly we see|create with the brain
but the mind creates mental images
either for or against the self
Give your eyes rest, give them a break daily
Let the internal feeling world overtake the external senses
Combining oneness
Life is gently alive...live gentle within
Find your groove Find your space to move
Find enough room to be you
Life desires & will make room for your
expansion through expression
Treat yourself well Living wellness
Able to show pure water to others
Able to offer a cup
A cup of health A cup of healing
Warmth for the soul
Care for you kindly...love you compassionately
Give from yourself to yourself
Give from yourself to the world
Universe gives to the generous
Be genuine Be sincere Be positive
Give yourself & the world space to be
Experience the individuals connection to the whole
Radiate peace love positivity from there
From where you are now your heart effects the world
Ask what is its impact...Ask what it could be

Good Thoughts

Truly find you here
I believe it's life's greatest quest
"Be in the world but not of it"
Your true essence may be linked to a realm
outside what we consider here
In this world though find yourself
Live & feel connected to what is naturally you
Attune to your rhythm Move at your pace
Life is dancing...Dance with it
Participate and play "leela"
Know know know tomorrow is a new day
Each moment a new moment
Always you ever evolving
Don't let blocks of time damn your river
Free the past story trying to rewrite itself now
Take back the pen...the power of living...
Freedom to create anew at anytime...
Release all limits in the future story
Breaking the damn of lack
Stop resisting your true power of presence
Now is always in balance
Bring yourself back to it
Stop the teetertawter of mind
Walk in faith the Earth rises to meet you
Step by Step by Step
Thank you Thank you Thank you
Life continues to unfold
The Universe continues to show
You continue to grow
Long live happily transcendent butterfly

Good Thoughts

1 6 6

Notice the ways in which you help others
Naturally...effortlessly...just who you are
Help the world in those ways
As you treat Home...Treat Earth
See the way you act & interact in a new light new manner
You are positive change in many ways already
What is it others want from you
Is that not your gift
For you yourself and them
You may not see with the eyes the impact
You already have on the planet
You effect the Universe in many ways
In dimensions unseeable
Keep radiating Keep creating
Keep on living forward moment to moment
Being positive in the world manifest
In the world you witness
Be the change...You are co-creator of it
You didn't just find yourself here...It was...It is...meant
Live the meaning...Embrace your importance
Accept your inborn divine worth
Walk humbly encounter yourself in all
Walk humbly encounter universe in all
Always here is all life
All power indescribable
Life source continuously present
Universal flow in harmonious movement
Reaching out calling out passing through you
Charge from its energy
Allow new Expansion new Levels new Matter

Good Thoughts

167

Oh life thank you
For everything...For every moment...For everyone...
For more than words can comprehend
For more than mind understands
For all opportunities For all possibilities
For all parallel realities
Thank you for divine time
Thank you for patience
When life feels stressful
When uncertainty toys with the mind
When solutions seem to hide
Thank you for hindsight
Thank you for clarity
Thank you for showing the way one step at a time
Thank you for bringing the ground up to kiss our feet
Thank you for ease, Thank you for dis ease
Thank you for signs something needs to change
Thank you for the power to change
Thank you for the courage to overcome
Thank you for the ability to transcend
Thank you for light...Thank you for love
Thank you for water...Thank you for air
Thank you for elements...Thank you for atoms
This world we find ourself in manifests from
within to without
As conscious observers, As conscious creators
We thank you life source for this inborn gifted mightiness
Thank you for the knowledge we have about
who & what we are
Thank you for the knowledge and mastery still on the way

Good Thoughts

1 6 8

Welcome uncertainty everyday
Life is always asking for your trust
Life is always asking you to release
Life asks for your surrender
Ceasing resistance
Re allowing energy to flow
We tend to hit plateaus energetically
Thinking we can go no further
Push no longer Reach no higher
Life asks you to rest
Re calibrate Re align Re balance
Going forward in a new manner
Usually lighter less baggage less to carry
Less limiting beliefs more self empowerment
Shed what is unnecessary
Examine all areas of life inner & outer
Lighten your life in the ways that means to you
Awareness increases upon letting go
Health increases upon letting go
Healing increases as energy flows
At the Quantum level the world is always moving
Don't constrict the movement of your life
Open the body Open the mind
Yoga is a key to unlock & unwind
Learn Unlearn Relearn
Live Love Appreciate
Gratefully Receive Let Go
Hurt Heal Help
Your life has been given to you as a gift,
as you live, so you give back your gift.

Good Thoughts

1 6 9

I wish a long healthy life to all.
Science, technology, medicine, mindset will drastically
extend the human lifespan. Presence & awareness in daily
life will become even more necessary, crucial, & vital.
Live fully in the present to enjoy all future presents.
Life is unpredictable, bring patience to all it has to offer.
Eat well, exercise, care for yourself for you may be here
longer than you expect. Be comfortable & confident in your
body, in your temple. Your soul chose this vessel, honor it.
Abstain from what you know is harmful.
Make empowering choices.
Release negativity, seek your own catharsis.
Follow your inner pull, be flexible & spontaneous.
Do what you believe you are supposed to do.
Re adjust when necessary
Don't let your ego get to attached
Your image, your identity, your work, are fluid and flowing.
Do not resist change, let go, no longer scratching, clawing,
grabbing hold to the past.
Live always now but define & find what live means for you...
In our world today 2018 these questions are necessary
What would you do if money did not matter?
What path would you enjoy walking?
If money did not *matter*...
Transcend primitive scarcity mindset
Transcend money scarcity mindset
Make decisions not based on restrictions

Settle Settle Settle Down
There is no rush, sit gather round
What is on its way, will be in due time
Be here...Be now...the world always now
Find & Found...Present & Presence
Keep on transcending the moment
that's the game...play along...
Focus your attention...Harness your alchemist powers
You are your shaman, you are your healer
You are your savior, as within as without
Control what you can control...let the rest go
Give in truly, sincerely, to the always present unknown...
Follow the beating of your heart in deep faith
Real Trust in yourself Real Trust in life
Dare to experience Dare to live Dare to accept the present
All is well here and now Explain otherwise?
.........that is past & future not now.
Always all is well now...learn and transcend
This too is will always will be passing
Appreciate & feel grateful for every breath
Hold gratitude in your heart
How did you get here?? You know...
Be humbled by the vastness of the stars & space...
There's no shame, you are the world
You are your world, treat yourself as such
Your world revolves around you...and others
but your center and their centers are within
The Universe is the whole of us pieces
Be proud to be alive...living history in the creating...

Here is a gift a gift I give I give you a piece of myself
A piece of my presence I give to you Now lives forevermore
First the words, settled in stone
Through and to the heart they find home
Here we sit, this time, this year
Words forever clear
Leave your mark on the Universe
Add your brushstrokes to the cosmic painting
Dare to be yourself as your honest truth
Find your core expression...serve the world
Find your giving that gives to you
Love yourself Love your mirror
Light up your world
Be at ease...ease those around you
There is always a rock a cornerstone
Set the example...Live Aligned
Be the rock...For you & those you love
There is much much unknown at play
The Power of Life is in us also greater than us
Live Honored Live humble Trust this great Power
Life gets better everyday
So do you | So can you | So will you
Thank you and welcome to being positive energy
For Radiating good vibrations
Thank you for living for the betterment of your life
& the lives of those & the world around you
You are the effect & the ripples
Save the world in your own way
Save yourself in your own way
Truly, Truthfully, express you in your living

Good Thoughts

I Love You

I Am Sorry

Please Forgive Me

Thank You

Sincerely